LEGACIES

from

ANCIENT ROME

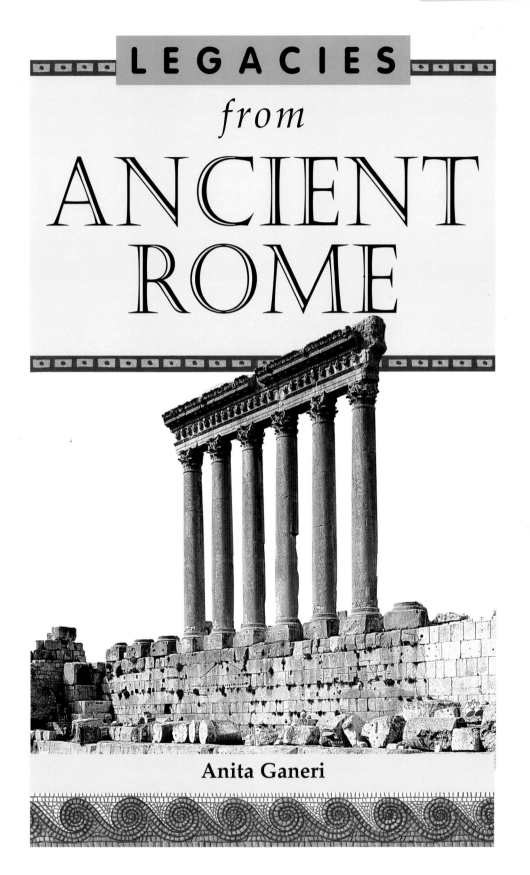

Anita Ganeri

Belitha Press

First published in the UK in 1999 by
Belitha Press Limited, London House,
Great Eastern Wharf, Parkgate Road,
London SW11 4NQ

ISBN 1 84138 065 2

British Library Cataloguing in Publication Data for
this book is available from the British Library.

Printed in China

Editor: Veronica Ross
Designer: Rosamund Saunders
Picture Researcher: Diana Morris
Consultant: Sallie Purkis
Illustrator: Jackie Harland

PHOTO CREDITS

THE DATES IN THIS BOOK
BC (Before Christ) is used with dates of events that
happened before the birth of Christ. AD (Anno Domini,
from the Latin for 'in the year of our Lord') is used with
dates of events that happened after the birth of Christ.
The letter c used in the text stands for the Latin word
circa, and means about.

Some of the more unfamiliar words used in this book
are explained in the glossary on page 30.

CONTENTS

INTRODUCTION

A legacy is something handed down from one person or generation to another. It may be an object, a lifestyle or a way of thinking. The Ancient Romans lived two thousand years ago, but the legacy of their culture lives on today. We still study and use their language and literature, and their ideas on government and administration have influenced legal and political systems all over the world. Many grand buildings copy Roman style, and many modern roads follow the routes of ancient Roman highways.

▲ This map shows the extent of the Roman Empire in the second century AD.

▼ The ruins of the Forum and the Colosseum can still be seen in the centre of the modern city of Rome.

IMPACT

Today Rome is the bustling capital of Italy as it was in ancient times. A visit to the city is like walking back through history. Everywhere you go there are magnificent ruins from the past. Among the most famous is the mighty Colosseum, where the citizens of ancient Rome flocked to watch gladiator fights and wild beast shows.

Who were the Romans?

The Ancient Romans were the people who lived in Rome, Italy. Gradually, the Romans conquered other lands and made them part of their empire, and from AD 212 all free-born people within the empire were Roman citizens. The Roman Empire lasted from the first century BC to the fifth century AD. At its height, in the first century AD, the Roman Empire covered about 30 countries, stretching from Britain in the north to Africa in the south, and from Spain in the west to Syria in the east. More than 50 million people lived within its borders. Roman culture spread far and wide and lasted long after the empire fell.

▲ Archaeologists at work, excavating the ruins of a Roman bath-house in London, England.

Roman history

Experts divide Roman history into two main parts. The first is called the republic. It began in about 510 or 509 BC when Tarquinius, the last king of Rome, was overthrown, and lasted until 27 BC when the first Roman emperor came to power. Rome was now called an empire.

How do we know?

We have plenty of information about Ancient Rome because so much evidence has survived. Archaeologists have excavated the ruins of Roman towns and forts. Many Roman buildings survive almost intact. Fragments of paintings, pottery, and objects such as jewellery and tools help us to build up a picture of what everyday life was like.

▶ These Roman leather shoes were found near the River Thames in London.

KEY DATES IN

| 700 BC | 500 BC | 100 BC | 50 BC |

c 753 BC The traditional date for the founding of Rome by Romulus, who became the city's first king after killing his brother, Remus.

312 BC Building of Rome's first great road, the Via Appia, begins. Rome's first aqueduct, the Aqua Appia, is also built. By AD 200, roads cover much of the Roman Empire.

73-71 BC Spartacus leads a slave rebellion. He is finally defeated by the Roman army.

59 BC Julius Caesar is elected consul of Rome.

264-241 BC The first Punic War is fought between Rome and Carthage.

58-49 BC Caesar's armies conquer Gaul (France) and invade Britain.

c 600 BC The Latin language is first written down in the alphabet still used today.

218-201 BC The second Punic War between Rome and Carthage. The great Carthaginian general Hannibal crosses the Alps by elephant to launch a surprise attack on the Romans.

44 BC On 15 March, Caesar is murdered in the Senate by a group of senators.

c 510 BC The last king of Rome is overthrown and Rome becomes a republic.

31 BC At the Battle of Actium, Octavian defeats Antony and Cleopatra, and takes control of Egypt.

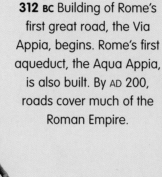

149-146 BC The third and final Punic War sees Carthage defeated and Rome the ruler of the lands around the Mediterranean Sea.

27 BC Octavian becomes Rome's first emperor and takes the title Augustus.

ANCIENT ROME

AD 20

AD 100

AD 500

AD 14 Death of Augustus. Tiberius becomes emperor.

AD 14-37 Rule of Tiberius.

AD 37-41 Rule of Caligula.

AD 41-54 Rule of Claudius.

AD 43 The Roman conquest of Britain begins.

AD 54-68 Rule of Nero.

AD 64 Rome is devastated by a great fire. Rumour says that it was started by Nero.

AD 69 The year of the four emperors. One of them, Vespasian, seizes power.

AD 69-79 Vespasian rules.

AD 79-81 Titus rules.

C AD 80 The Colosseum in Rome is opened by Titus. This huge amphitheatre is used to stage gladiator fights. It can seat about 50,000 people.

AD 81-96 Domitian rules.

AD 96-98 Nerva rules.

AD 98-117 Trajan rules. Under Trajan, the empire reaches its greatest size.

AD 117-138 Hadrian rules. He orders the building of frontier walls in Britain, Germany and Africa.

AD 165-167 Plague and famine sweep through the empire.

AD 284-305 Diocletian divides the empire into two parts – east and west. Diocletian rules in the east.

AD 312-337 Constantine rules. He reunites the empire (though it is later divided again) and founds a new capital city in the east, called Constantinople (modern-day Istanbul). On his deathbed, he is baptized into the Christian faith. Christianity later becomes the official religion of the Roman Empire.

AD 410 Rome is ransacked by Gothic armies from Germany.

AD 455 Rome is sacked again by the Vandals.

AD 476 The western empire falls and the last western emperor, Romulus Augustus, is overthrown. The eastern empire survives until 1453. It becomes known as the Byzantine Empire.

THE STORY OF ROME

◄ *An Etruscan statue of the god Apollo.*

The city of Rome is thought to have been founded in about 753 BC. It began as a group of villages built on seven hills beside the River Tiber. The villages were well placed for trade, and soon grew wealthy and merged to become one large town. Early Rome was ruled by kings and grew into a great city. The kings were Etruscans, the people who lived in north-west Italy. Their rule continued until 510 or 509 BC, when the last king was driven out of the city. Rome then became a republic.

FAMOUS PEOPLE

Legend says that Rome was founded by two brothers, Romulus and Remus, the twin sons of Mars, god of war. Left to die by the River Tiber, they were looked after by a she-wolf. The brothers built a city on the Palatine Hill near the spot where they were found. But they quarrelled and Remus was killed. Romulus became the first king of Rome and gave the city its name.

Romulus and Remus, and the she-wolf who saved them.

The Roman republic

During the republic, Rome was ruled by two consuls elected each year from a group of important citizens called the Senate. Through hard fighting and clever politics, Rome quickly grew in power and size. By 260 BC Rome controlled much of Italy and began its conquest abroad. In 264 BC a clash with the powerful city of Carthage in North Africa led to a series of terrible wars. Carthage was finally defeated in 146 BC, and soon the whole Mediterranean region came under Roman rule.

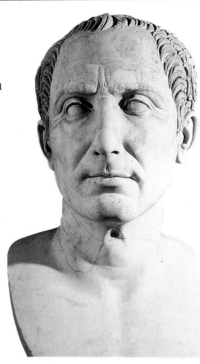

◀ Julius Caesar (c 100-44 BC) was a brilliant politician and soldier. Many of the books he wrote are still studied today.

IMPACT

While the western part of the empire collapsed, the eastern empire lived on. It is known as the Byzantine Empire. Its capital was the city of Constantinople in Turkey, which today is called Istanbul. Art and culture continued to flourish, but links with Rome were gradually broken, and Greek was spoken instead of Latin. The Byzantine Empire survived until AD 1453 when it was conquered by the Ottoman Turks.

From Republic to Empire

In 59 BC, the great general Julius Caesar was elected consul. But soon he had defeated his rivals and ruled on his own as a dictator. On 15 March 44 BC, Caesar was murdered by a group of senators who were afraid of his growing power. Civil war followed and the republic collapsed. In 27 BC, Caesar's adopted son Octavian seized power and set about restoring peace and stability. He became Rome's first emperor and was given the title Augustus, which means 'revered one' in Latin.

Decline and fall

Rome was ruled by emperors for the next 500 years. But towards the end of the second century AD, problems began for the empire with rising taxes, foreign invasions and squabbles over power. In AD 285, Emperor Diocletian divided the empire into west and east, each with its own emperor. But in AD 410 Rome was ransacked by the Goths and the western empire collapsed. The last western emperor Romulus Augustus was deposed in AD 476.

The Santa Sophia in Istanbul, a famous Byzantine church.

RULING ROME

During the republic Rome was governed by the Senate. Each year the Senate elected two senior officials, called consuls, who managed the affairs of the Senate and the army. Later, power passed to the emperor who became the sole ruler in Rome. Abroad, Roman territory was divided into provinces, each with its own governor. The governor commanded the army stationed in his province, collected taxes and was responsible for keeping law and order.

Napoleon Bonaparte, emperor of France.

◀ Inside the Senate of the American government in Washington DC.

The emperors of Rome were both good and bad. After an illness, Caligula (ruled AD 37-41) went mad, declared himself a god and is said to have wanted to have his favourite horse elected consul. His cruelty and extravagance made him very unpopular, and he was murdered by soldiers in AD 41.

Senate elections

The Senate was originally a group of 100 men, though this later increased to 600. Each year, Roman citizens voted to elect senators to become government officials. The most important of these were the two consuls. As a sign of their rank, only senators were allowed to wear togas with a purple trim. In the USA today, one of the two main houses of the central government is still called the Senate and its members senators.

The emperors

During the Roman Empire supreme power over Rome and all its territories belonged to the emperor. He was also the *Pontifex Maximus*, or chief priest. The first Roman emperor, Augustus (ruled 27 BC–AD 14) was a brilliant politician and a highly successful ruler. He brought peace and prosperity back to Rome after years of chaos and civil war. The month of August was named in his honour. He was succeeded by his step-son, Tiberius.

▲ A Roman gold coin bearing the head of the Emperor Augustus.

In the army

Rome's rapid expansion and success was largely due to its army, the best armed and disciplined in the ancient world. The army was organized into divisions, or legions, of about 5000 men who joined up for 20-25 years. Apart from fighting wars to extend the empire, legionaries also guarded frontiers, kept the peace, and supervised the buildings of roads and forts across the empire (see pages 20-21, 24-25). It was a very hard life and soldiers had to be tough.

▶ A statue of a lictor, an official who accompanied a Roman magistrate and carried a bundle of rods which symbolized power.

LAW AND SOCIETY

Many of the legal systems used around the world today, such as the French legal system, are based on Ancient Roman law. Law and order was vital for the smooth running of the Roman Empire. There was a vast number of laws and ways of interpreting them. These were standardized by Emperor Hadrian in the second century AD. Later the laws were reformed by Emperor Justinian (ruled AD 527-565) and became known as the Justinian Code. This formed the basis of law throughout western Europe.

▼ *French lawyers outside the main law courts in Paris. French law is based on Ancient Roman law.*

On trial

In Rome, trials were held in the basilica, the largest, finest building in the forum. As today, suspects were tried by a jury. In serious cases the jury consisted of up to 75 citizens, not the 12 we have today. The accused person might pay a lawyer to defend him. Good lawyers were highly respected and in great demand. Everyone spoke, and then the jury voted on whether the accused was guilty or not. Then the judge announced the verdict and the punishment.

FAMOUS PEOPLE

One of the most famous lawyers in Ancient Rome was Cicero (106-43 BC). Educated in Rome and Athens, his stirring speeches in the law courts earned him a reputation as the greatest public speaker of his day. Many of his speeches and letters were written down and are still read today. His style of speaking was copied for many years after his death.

Cicero was a great writer, as well as a powerful lawyer.

Plebs and patricians

Roman society was divided into citizens, who could vote in elections and serve in the army, and slaves. Slaves had no rights or status. There were three classes of citizens – patricians, *equites* and plebeians. Patricians were rich aristocrats who held the highest political and legal posts. Equites were wealthy businessmen. Plebeians were ordinary citizens.

A slave's life

Many slaves were prisoners of war brought to Rome to be sold at market. Some slaves suffered very badly at the hands of cruel masters. Others were treated well and paid a wage, which enabled them to buy their freedom. Slaves were often released on the death of their masters and given the status of freedmen. Government slaves were set to work on building sites and down the mines. A lucky few became civil servants.

▲ *Roman slaves sometimes wore tags, like dogs.*

LETTERS AND NUMBERS

Could you speak like an Ancient Roman? You might be surprised. Many of the words we use everyday in English come from Latin, the language spoken in Ancient Rome. For example, video is Latin for I see, and decimal comes from the Latin for ten. Many place-names have Roman roots, for example, the Latin name for London was Londinium. Place-names ending in chester come from the Latin *castrum*, or camp. Even when Ancient Rome fell, Latin was kept alive by the Roman Catholic Church as its official language. Latin is still taught and studied in some schools today.

▼ A famous painting from Pompeii. The woman is holding a type of Roman pen called a stylus. It was used for scratching letters on wax.

Latin letters

Although many different languages were spoken throughout the Roman Empire, the official language was Latin. This helped unite the people of the empire and made trade and communications much easier. The Latin alphabet had 22 letters. There was no W or Y; I and J were both written as I, and U and V as V. Letters were made up of straight lines to make them easier to carve on stone, wax or metal. The alphabet we use to write English today is based on the alphabet used to write Latin.

▲ A gold shield with an inscription written in Latin.

◄ A schoolroom scene showing a lesson in progress.

Learning to write

From the age of six or seven to eleven, Roman schoolchildren spent most of their lessons learning to read and write Latin. They scratched out their letters on wooden boards, covered in wax. If they went wrong, they simply smoothed the wax over. Some Romans also learned Greek.

Roman numerals

What year is it? MCMXCIX. This is the year 1999 written in Roman numerals. Letters stood for numbers, so I = 1, V = 5, X = 10, L = 50, C = 100, D = 500, M = 1000. These were added together or subtracted to make bigger or smaller numbers. Large numbers were very clumsy and complicated, which made doing sums very hard! Roman numerals are still used on some clock and watch faces.

◄ Roman numerals on a clock face.

LITERATURE AND IDEAS

M uch of our knowledge of Ancient Rome comes from written sources, such as letters, speeches, histories, poems and plays. All of them give us a precious insight into how the Romans thought and lived. Many of these works are still studied, and Roman ideas continue to influence our lives.

Famous poets

The two greatest Roman poets were Virgil (70-19 BC) and Ovid (43 BC-AD 18). Virgil's epic poem, the *Aeneid*, tells the story of Aeneas, a Trojan prince. When the Greeks destroyed Troy, during the Trojan War, Aeneas escaped to Italy where his descendants founded the city of Rome. Ovid's most famous work is *Metamorphoses*, 15 books of poetry, in which the characters change into animals and plants.

▼ *This book illustration shows a banquet scene from Virgil's Aeneid. His poem has inspired many later works of art.*

Christianity

At first the Romans tried to stamp out Christianity and many early Christians were persecuted or killed. But in the fourth century AD, Emperor Constantine made Christianity the official religion of Rome, and many Roman buildings were converted into churches. In western Europe, Rome has remained the centre of the Roman Catholic Church.

FAMOUS PEOPLE

The Romans loved going to the theatre. Their favourite plays were comedies. The most famous comic writer was Plautus (c 254–184 BC). Only 21 of Plautus' 130 plays survive, all based on Greek comedies. They were full of puns, plays on words, and larger-than-life characters, and were hugely popular with Roman audiences.

Roman actors getting ready to make their appearance on stage.

IMPACT

Events from Roman history were the inspiration behind some of William Shakespeare's most famous plays. *Julius Caesar* tells the story of Caesar's murder. In *Antony and Cleopatra*, Mark Antony, one of the later rulers of Rome, neglects his duties because of his love for Cleopatra, queen of Egypt. *Coriolanus* is a great soldier who is elected consul but becomes very unpopular and is murdered. These plays have been translated into hundreds of languages, and performed all over the world.

A scene from a modern performance of Julius Caesar.

Changing the calendar

Our calendar is called the Gregorian calendar. It came into use in the sixteenth century, but is based on the Julian calendar, devised by Julius Caesar. Originally a Roman year lasted for 120 days, divided into four months. This meant that it quickly fell out of step with the seasons. To bring it back into line, Caesar ordered the year 46 BC to last for 445 days. After that, each year was 365 days long with an extra day every four years. This extra day, 29 February, still survives in every leap year.

◄ *The Julian calendar, with the months, days and weeks marked out with pegs.*

BRILLIANT BUILDERS

The Romans were brilliant builders and engineers. Many of their buildings were so well made that they survive today. The Romans copied many of their ideas about architecture from the Greeks, but they also developed their own techniques. One of their most important building discoveries was concrete. This allowed them to build on a very grand scale and to leave a long-lasting legacy.

▼ *Part of the peristyle that once ran around the Temple of Jupiter in Baalbeck, Lebanon.*

Public buildings

The most famous Roman buildings were the grand public buildings found in every city, such as basilicas, temples, baths and amphitheatres. These were often paid for by the emperor to show off his wealth and power. The Romans copied Greek temple architecture very closely, in particular the row of columns around the outside of the temple. This was called a *peristyle*. Each temple was dedicated to one of the official gods or goddesses, or to the emperor who was worshipped as a god.

Making concrete

Sometime in the second century BC, the Romans discovered how to make concrete from volcanic rocks and rubble. This allowed them to build much bigger structures. Before this, the main building material was stone. But this would have been much too heavy to build the Romans' famous domes and arches.

▲ This Roman bridge arches over the river in Cordoba, Spain.

FAMOUS PEOPLE

One of the greatest architects of Ancient Rome was a man called Vitruvius (c 70 BC– early first century AD). He wrote a ten-volume handbook called *De Architectura* (*About Architecture*), the only work of its kind to have survived. In it, Vitruvius gives detailed information about all aspects of Roman engineering and town-planning, including building techniques, materials and decoration.

IMPACT

Many later builders followed Roman designs. The Arc de Triomphe in Paris was built between 1806-1836 to celebrate Napoleon's victories in battle. It was a copy of a Roman triumphal arch, built by the emperors to celebrate their great victories. Several ancient arches still stand in Rome, including the Arch of Constantine near the Colosseum.

The Arc de Triomphe in Paris, France.

Arches and domes

Roman builders were the first to use large arches. This allowed them to build bridges and amphitheatres. Domes were made by crossing several arches over each other. The finest is the Pantheon in Rome. It was built as a temple to all the gods in 27 BC. The dome measures 43 metres high and 43 metres across. It was made by pouring concrete over a wooden framework. In the seventh century AD, the Pantheon was turned into a church. It is still used as a church today.

▲ The Pantheon in Rome. Light pours through a hole in the top of the dome.

WALLS AND WATERWORKS

The Romans also put their building skills to practical use. In the cities, huge amounts of water were used and a good, regular supply was vital. This is where Roman engineering shone. To bring water into the cities from mountain springs, the Romans built aqueducts. Some were very long – the aqueduct bringing water to Pompeii started 40 kilometres away. Peace and security were also vital, and huge, stone walls were built along the frontiers to keep invaders out. Some are still standing today.

▲ The Pont du Gard is a huge, three-storey Roman aqueduct. Every day it supplied 20,000 tonnes of water to the French city of Nîmes.

Water supply

An aqueduct is a pipe or channel for carrying water. In fact, aqueduct is Latin for bringing water. Sometimes the pipes were laid underground. Where they had to cross rivers or valleys, they were set into large bridges. The water flowed into a reservoir, and was then distributed around the city through a complex system of lead, clay or wooden pipes. Few homes had their own water supplies. People fetched water from public fountains in the street.

▲ The city of Bath in England is famous for its Roman baths.

Roman baths

In Roman times, having a bath was a popular pastime. Every town had a public bath-house, where people could bathe, exercise and chat to their friends. The baths were not like the bathtub you have at home. You bathed first in a hot pool, then plunged into a cold one.

IMPACT

In his *De Architectura* (see page 19), Vitruvius wrote the first description of a crane used by Roman builders. The crane was made of wood, and powered by a wheel called a treadmill. Inside, slaves walked round and round, making the wheel turn. The turning wheel pulled on a rope which lifted a heavy block of stone from the ground. Today cranes are commonplace on building sites all over the world.

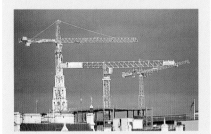

Modern-day cranes on a building site.

FAMOUS PEOPLE

An official called the *curator aquarum* (keeper of water) was appointed to look after the water supply. In AD 97, the former governor of Britain, Frontinus, was made *curator aquarum* of Rome. It was a very tough job. Not only did he have to make sure the city had enough water – about 1000 million litres a day – but he also had to try to stop dishonest people tapping into the pipes illegally, without paying any water tax.

Hadrian's Wall

The best preserved Roman wall is Hadrian's Wall in Britain. Built between AD 122-129, it runs for nearly 130 kilometres across northern England. Sixteen forts were built into the wall, each with room for about 500 soldiers. There were look-out towers at regular intervals. The wall was built by Roman soldiers in Britain who were also responsible for its upkeep.

▲ Hadrian's wall was built at the emperor's command to mark England's northern boundary.

TOWN PLANNING

Roman cities were carefully planned and built on a grid plan with straight streets at right angles to each other. The Romans borrowed the idea from the Greeks. The streets divided the buildings into blocks, a pattern followed in some modern cities, such as New York, USA. A wall was built around the city to mark the boundary. Roman cities were busy, crowded places. By the first century AD more than one million people lived in Rome. Visitors from the provinces were astonished by Rome's size and the magnificence of its buildings.

IMPACT

Graffiti means words or drawings scribbled on walls, often as a sign of protest. But graffiti is not a modern invention. In Pompeii, the walls were covered in graffiti. Some listed market days in neighbouring towns or advertised games in the amphitheatre. One message read: 'I am surprised, O Wall, that you have not fallen down with the weight of all this scribbled rubbish.'

Graffiti on a wall in New York.

▼ *A drawing of how Ancient Rome might have looked.*

Rich and poor

Wealthy Romans lived in large town houses and had villas in the country where they went to escape the city. Ordinary people lived in cramped blocks of flats, called *insulae*, with no running water, drains or toilets. The ground floor was often taken up by shops. The wooden *insulae* were badly built and frequently collapsed or burned to the ground.

▶ *A model of Emperor Hadrian's country villa at Tivoli, outside Rome.*

FAMOUS PEOPLE

In AD 64, Rome was destroyed by a terrible fire. Rumour said that Emperor Nero (ruled AD 54-68) started the fire himself and even sang and played his lyre as he watched Rome burn. Afterwards Nero built himself an amazing new palace called the Golden House. It was 25 times the size of the Colosseum which was later built in its place.

The forum

At the centre of each Roman town was a large, open space called the forum. It was used as a marketplace and a meeting place where people met to discuss business and affairs of state. Around the forum were public buildings, such as the basilica, or law court, the *curia*, or Senate house, and the temples to the gods. Today we use the word forum to mean a place where people can openly debate their views.

▼ *The ruins of some of the streets and houses of Pompeii.*

Pompeii

On 24 August AD 79, Mount Vesuvius, a volcano near Naples, Italy, erupted and buried the town of Pompeii in ash. Thousands of people were killed. More than 1500 years later, workers building a water tunnel discovered the remains of the town. Serious excavations began in 1748 and today almost all of the town has been unearthed. The ash which smothered the town also froze it in time. Many objects were perfectly preserved, including houses, mosaics, paintings and even loaves of bread.

ROMAN ROADS

The Romans were the greatest road builders of the ancient world. By about AD 200, they had built a network of roads, stretching for 85,000 kilometres to every corner of the empire. The roads were mainly used for moving troops around. The first main road was the Via Appia, which ran from south-east Rome to Capua. Begun in 312 BC, it took a hundred years to build. Even though Roman road-building skills were lost at the end of the empire, the roads were so well made that many survive today. Some are still in use. Others form the basis of modern roads and railway lines.

FAMOUS PEOPLE

Where the Via Appia led out of Rome, the road was lined with tombs and monuments. This was because burials were not allowed within the sacred boundary of the city walls. One of the most famous to survive is the large tomb built for a Roman noblewoman, Cecilia Metella. Her father and husband were wealthy patricians and successful generals during the republic, but very little else is known about her.

▶ *The Via Appia as it looks today. It was the first in a vast network of Roman roads.*

How a road was built

Roman roads followed the shortest, straightest, most direct route possible. A trench was dug about 1.5 metres deep, and filled with layers of sand, rubble and cement. Then flat stone slabs were laid on top. Roads were built with a raised curve, or camber, and with ditches down each side. This helped any rainwater to drain away.

▲ The tombstone of a Roman postmaster. It shows a carriage of the cursus publicus.

IMPACT

Our word mile comes from *mille*, the Latin word for a thousand. A Roman mile was a thousand paces, or about 1460 metres long. A pace was two soldier's strides. A modern mile measures just over 1609 metres. Every mile was marked by a stone. In the forum in Rome, Emperor Augustus set up a golden milestone. All roads ran towards it, giving rise to the saying that all roads lead to Rome.

Delivering the post

Apart from the army, the roads were used by traders and by the riders of the *cursus publicus*, the official government postal service. Relays of riders, on horseback or in horse-drawn carriages, carried messages all over the empire. Every 30-40 kilometres along the road was a post station where riders could rest or change horses.

Wheels and gauges

The wheels on most Roman carts and chariots were set about 143 centimetres apart. This measurement is called a gauge. Once enough wheels had worn grooves into the new roads, this became the standard gauge, and from then on all carts were built with wheels this width apart.

A Roman milestone.

▶ Some modern railway lines follow the routes of Roman roads.

ROMAN ART

Wealthy Romans were very fond of fine paintings, mosaics and statues which they used to decorate their villas. Some of these survive today. They are usually based on everyday life or show scenes or figures from mythology. In the fifteenth century, European artists became fascinated by the Roman way of life and were inspired by Roman art and style. This period was called the Renaissance. The word means rebirth because it seemed that Roman style had been reborn.

FAMOUS PEOPLE

In the first century AD, three Greek sculptors from Rhodes, Hagesander, Athanadorus and Polydorus, created one of the most famous sculptures of Ancient Rome. This great marble statue shows the Trojan priest, Laocoon, and his sons struggling with a sea serpent. It was discovered in 1506 near the site of Nero's Golden House (see page 23) and is now on display in the Vatican.

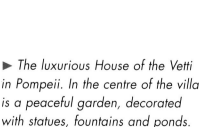

► *The luxurious House of the Vetti in Pompeii. In the centre of the villa is a peaceful garden, decorated with statues, fountains and ponds.*

Wall paintings

Walls were decorated with colourful paintings called frescoes. These were painted on while the plaster was still wet, which stopped the colours fading. Frescoes often showed country or garden scenes, or gods and goddesses. Some were incredibly realistic still life pictures, showing a bowl of fruit or a wine glass.

Mosaic making

The most famous art to survive from Roman times is mosaic making. Mosaics were used to cover floors. They were made from thousands of tiny pieces of coloured stone, called tesserae, each about 5 millimetres square. These were laid in wet plaster by expert mosaic makers. It was a very skilful job. Sometimes, the central picture would be made up in the workshop then taken to the villa. Then a patterned border was added.

▶ *A fresco of Flora, goddess of Spring.*

IMPACT

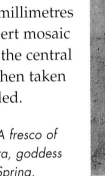

Many later artists used Roman myths and legends as inspiration for their work. One of the greatest Italian painters of the Renaissance, Raphael (1483-1520), based his famous painting *The Fire in the Borgo* on an episode from Virgil's *Aeneid*. It shows Aeneas fleeing from Troy, carrying his father on his back. Raphael's paintings are considered some of the finest works of art of all time.

Aeneas carrying his father.

St Peter's Basilica

Today, the Vatican City in Rome is the centre of the Roman Catholic Church. Its most splendid church is St Peter's Basilica. Based on an ancient design, the first church was built in about AD 349. It was rebuilt in the sixteenth century, under the guidance of its chief architect, the great Renaissance artist and sculptor, Michelangelo. One of the largest churches in the world, its huge dome is 132 metres high.

▼ *The front of St Peter's Basilica in the Vatican City, Rome. Inside it is just as ornate as it is outside.*

HOME COMFORTS

Roman mosaics, frescoes and writings tell us a great deal about how the Romans lived their daily lives. Rich and poor people lived very different lives. Rich people lived comfortably in splendid homes with good food, fine clothes and slaves to wait on them. Life was much harder if you were poor. Then you had to work hard and had little time for leisure. Some of the Romans' most interesting legacies have come from their everyday lives.

FAMOUS PEOPLE

Marcus Apicius was a Roman writer whose famous cookery book still survives. Written in the first century AD, it gives details of how to make many Roman dishes. A modern translation of Apicius' cookbook was published in 1984 so modern cooks could try out Roman recipes. Try one yourself. To make stuffed dates you need to stone the dates and stuff them with nuts, pine kernels and ground pepper. Roll them in salt and fry in warm honey, then serve.

▶ A fresco showing a wealthy Roman woman playing the lyre. Rich Romans lived very comfortable lives.

Central heating

The Romans invented underfloor central heating in the first century AD. It was called a hypocaust. The floor of a building was raised on brick pillars. A fire was lit and its heat flowed up under the floor, heating it gently. Spaces were left in the walls so that the heat could circulate around the room. In warm places it was mainly used to heat bath-houses. In colder climates it was found in town houses and country villas.

▲ The foundations of a hypocaust from the Roman palace of Fishbourne in southern England.

Herbal medicine

Herbal medicine has been used for centuries all over the world. Roman doctors used many potions and ointments made from plants or herbs. These included lemon balm for headaches and basil for stomachaches. Some herbs were mixed with wine to make cough mixture. The Roman writer Pliny lists 40 medicines with mustard as the main ingredient. Garlic was thought to be very good for you, just as it is today.

Beware of the dog!

▼ A snack bar in Pompeii. Pottery jars sunk into the counter contained wine and hot food.

Fast food

People who lived in *insulae* did not have kitchens to cook in. Instead, they bought hot food from stalls, called *thermopolia*. Ordinary people ate a simple diet of bread, cheese, olives and beans. Most people drank wine mixed with water. Wealthy Romans held feasts, serving delicacies such as flamingo, dormouse and larks' tongues! Guests lay on couches and ate with their fingers, which were wiped between courses by slaves.

GLOSSARY

amphitheatre An oval or circular building in which gladiator fights and wild-beast shows took place. Amphitheatres were built all over the Roman Empire. The most famous is the Colosseum in Rome.

aqueduct A pipe or channel for carrying water. Some aqueducts were laid underground. Others were set into large bridges so that they could run across valleys and rivers.

archaeologist A person who studies human history by excavating and examining ruins and remains, such as ancient cities, burial sites and artefacts, such as pots and tools.

aristocrats Members of the ruling or upper class in a society. In Rome, they were called patricians.

basilica A large public building in a Roman town, often in the forum. It was used as a town hall and law court, and sometimes as offices and shops.

boundary A line around a city or town that marks the limit of the city or town.

citizen A Roman man who had the right to vote. Eventually all Roman men were granted citizenship apart from slaves.

civil war A war fought between two groups of people from the same city or country.

consul During the republic, the most important official in the government. Two consuls were elected each year. They looked after the Senate and commanded the army.

culture A country or people's achievements in the arts, sciences and technology.

depose To remove someone from office, for example a king or ruler.

descendants Your relatives and family who come after you.

dictator A ruler who has absolute power. Julius Caesar ruled Rome as a dictator.

empire A large and powerful state, often made up of several countries and territories. It is ruled over by a single leader called an emperor or empress.

excavate To dig up or unearth. It is often used to describe the way in which archaeologists find artefacts from the past which have been hidden underground.

frontier Another word for the border between one country or empire and another.

gladiator A former slave, prisoner or criminal who fought to the death to entertain the Roman public.

Goths People from northern Europe who attacked Roman territory many times and ransacked Rome itself in AD 410.

governor The ruler of a Roman province who was appointed by and had to answer to the Roman emperor.

grid A pattern of straight lines that criss-cross each other at right angles. Roman cities were laid out in a grid pattern.

interpret To bring out or explain the meaning of something.

lyre An ancient musical stringed instrument that looked like a harp but was small enough to hold in the hand.

magistrate A person concerned with the administration of the law.

medieval To do with the period of history in Europe which is called the Middle Ages. It lasted from about AD 500 to 1400.

monarchy A state or country ruled by a monarch, for example a king, queen, emperor or empress. The monarch may rule alone or with a government.

mythology A collection of stories that are not based in historical fact, but deal with supernatural characters, such as gods and heroes, their lives and their actions.

ornate Highly decorated

Ottoman Turks People from Turkey who founded a great empire in 1290 which overthrew the Byzantine Empire in AD 1453.

patron Someone who gives money and support to another person, such as an artist or writer, to help their work.

persecute To harm someone or even kill them because of their beliefs.

province Roman territory outside Rome was divided into provinces. Each province was ruled by a governor.

ransacked When a place such as a city is destroyed, its buildings burned or knocked down and goods and property stolen.

reform To make something or someone work or behave better.

republic A state or country that is ruled by elected leaders chosen by the people, rather than by an unelected king.

reputation What other people think about a person's character and the way he or she behaves.

reservoir A place where water is stored. It may be a tank or a large lake.

right-angle An angle of 90° made up by two straight lines meeting, for example in a shape such as a square or triangle.

Roman Catholic Church One of the largest groups of Christians, led by the Pope in the Vatican City, Rome.

Senate The group of officials that ruled Rome. During the republic, the Senate was very powerful. Later, much of their power passed to the emperor.

senator A member of the Senate.

species A group of animals that is closely related.

symbolize To stand for or signal something else. For example, the crown worn by a king or queen might be a symbol of power.

Vandals People from northern Europe who ransacked Rome in AD 455. Today we use the word vandal to mean someone who causes trouble or damage.

INDEX